Mother F*cking Girl Power

by katie yackley moore

also by katie yackley moore

Happy Broken Crayons

You are a Warrior

We are Family

Dream a Bigger Dream

This one is for the hornets
Caitlin, Carrie & Jen

thank you for always pitching
the red tent

Authors note:

For as long as I can remember, I have been obsessed with quotes. When I was a young girl, I read "Life's Little Instruction Book" until the spine was torn and tattered. I wrote its quotes on index cards and hung them on my lipstick pink walls. Throughout high school and college I was infatuated with great words stitched together in the most poetic ways. I loved the feeling of reading something that felt like it was written just for you, that awakening that whispers, "This. This is what you needed to hear today."

As time trembled on and my babies came into the world, I lost a little bit of that magical love affair of reading. I was just so damn tired. I was pulled under by the weight of adulthood. I fell hard for my children and wanted to embrace every ounce of motherhood, as it should be, but I wish I had taken a little more care of myself in those all-consuming early days, weeks, years. I fell out of love with me. In the fall of 2016, my husband and I separated. This was years in the making but that didn't make it any less hard.

I began a new love affair. With Pinterest.

When my children were tucked in bed that became my time to rediscover the words I yearned to hear. Quick, glorious reminders of the strength of women that have been through hell and the embodiment that we all have the grit and grace to keep carrying on. I drank in these words as though were my salvation and between them and my girlfriends and my family, they actually were. The power of these words that I was not alone and I was braver than I ever was going to give myself credit for were enough to keep me showing up every single day, ready for life and whatever trench I found myself slipping down or climbing out of.

This is that collection of quotes. These women are my superheroes. The ones that remind us that we have mother fucking girl power even when we can't see it and that there is a badass within us all.

Here's to the journey. We've so got this. Thank you for being here.

also every quote that does not have the author's name is in no way intentional, it just means that unfortunately no author was listed with those words that I can give credit to so those are just known as "unknown." And I tried to emulate the poetic integrity of the quotes and print words and punctuation just as the writers intended them to look so that is why certain pieces are all in lowercase and why line breaks appear as they do.

Thank you for your understanding... xoxo

I'm with the dirty
mouth girls.
The ones with bare
feet, brilliant minds,
messy hair, wild
hearts and feisty
spirits.
The ones who aren't
afraid to speak up and
who live for doing
what they've been told
is impossible.

You had the power all
along,
my dear.

Glinda, The Good Witch

One morning she woke up
different.
Done with trying to
figure out who was with
her, against her, or
walking down the middle
because they didn't have
the guts to pick a side.
She was done with
anything that didn't
bring her peace. She
realized that opinions
were a dime a dozen,
validation was for
parking, and loyalty
wasn't a word but a
lifestyle. It was this day
that her life changed.
Not because of a man or a
job but because she
realized that life is way
too short to leave the key
to your happiness in
someone else's pocket.

I did what my
conscience told
me to do.
And you can't fail
if you do that.

Anita Hill

Make it happen sister.
Shock the hell
out of everyone.

I am a woman with
thoughts and
questions and shit
to say.
I say if I'm beautiful.
I say if I'm strong.
You will not determine
my story-
I will.

Amy Schumer

This is the part of my
life where I silently
remove myself from
anyone who hurts
me more than
they love me,
drains me more than
they replenish me,
brings me more stress
than they do peace,
and tries to stunt my
growth rather than
clap for it.
I think that I've done
more than enough
talking and trying to
make things work with
certain people.
I'm done.

CiCi B

It's ok if you fall
down and lose
your spark.
Just make sure that
when you get back up,
you rise
as the whole
damn fire.

Comparison is one
long, agonizing death
and does not interest
me at all.

Kristen Bell

Now, every time I
witness a strong
person,
I want to know:
What dark did you
conquer in your story?
Mountains do not rise
without earthquakes.

Katherine MacKenett

Do not be afraid
to give yourself
everything you've
ever wanted
in life.

Keep your heels, head
and
standards high.

Coco Chanel

don't be someone's "sometimes"

Bridgett Devoue

I don't chase people
anymore.
I learned that
I'm here,
and I'm important.
I'm not going to run
after people to prove
that I matter.

I refuse to live
as half of myself
because other people
can't handle all of me.

Rachel Hollis

Know this:
you can start over
each morning.

Don't feel stupid if
you don't like what
everyone else
pretends to love.

Emma Watson

I knew who I was
this morning,
but I've changed
a few times since
then.

Alice in Wonderland

Never apologize for
being a powerful
fucking woman.

You get in life what
you have the courage
to ask for.

Oprah Winfrey

Darling,
you feel heavy because
you are too full of
truth.

Open your mouth more.
Let the truth exist
somewhere other than
inside your body.

Della Hicks-Wilson

Misery is a choice.

Owning your story
is the bravest thing
you'll ever do.

Brene Brown

You don't have to move
mountains.
Simply fall
in love with life.
Be a tornado
of happiness,
gratitude and
acceptance.
You will change
the world just by
being a warm, kind
hearted human being.

Anita Krizzan

I asked God if it was okay
to be melodramatic
and she said yes
I asked her it if was
okay to be short
and she said it sure is
I asked her if I could
wear nail polish
or not wear nail polish
and she said honey
she calls me that
sometimes
she said you can do just
exactly
what you want to
Thanks God I said
And is it even okay if I
don't paragraph
my letters
Sweetcakes God said
who knows where she
picked that up
what I'm telling you is
Yes Yes Yes

Kaylin Haught

Occupation:
aspiring beam of
light.

Even when someone
gets to looking
like she should be so
proud of herself;
instead she's like,
'I could be another
three pounds less.
I could be a little
taller and have
bigger lips.'
Where does it end?
You just have to say,
'It's pretty damn good.
I am right here at the
moment and I'm okay
with it.
I've got other things
to think about.'

Melissa McCarthy

You must read to your
children and you must
hug your children and
you must love
your children.
Your success
as a family,
our success
as a society,
depends
not on what happens
in the White House,
but on what happens
inside your house.

Barbara Bush

Britney made it
through 2007.
You can make it
through today.

Life shrinks
or expands in
proportion
to one's courage.

Anais Nin

Money won't buy
you happiness,
but it will bring
you freedom.

@bossbabe.inc

You are beautiful
because you let
yourself feel,
and that is a brave
thing indeed.

Shinji Moon

I stopped waiting
for the light at the
end of the tunnel
and lit
that bitch myself.

No one can
make you feel
inferior
without
your consent.

Eleanor Roosevelt

I love to see
a young girl
go out and grab
the world by the
lapels.
Life's a bitch.
You've got to go out
and kick ass.

Maya Angelou

Some of the most
wonderful people are
the ones who don't fit
into boxes.

I'm not impressed by
money, social status,
or job titles.
I'm impressed
by the way someone
treats other
human beings.

Beware the person who
stabs you and then
tells the world
they're the one
who's bleeding.

Jill Blakeway

Don't think about what
can happen in a month.
Don't think about what
can happen in a year.
Just focus on the
twenty-four hours
in front of you and do
what you can to get
closer to where
you want to be.

Life is a party.
Dress like it.

Audrey Hepburn

I always did
something I was
a little not ready
to do.
I think that's how
you grow.
When there's that
moment of
"Wow. I'm not really
sure I can do this,"
and you push through
those moments, that's
when you have a
breakthrough.

Marissa Mayer

the world
gives you
so much pain
and here you are
making gold of it

there is nothing purer than
that-
rupi kaur

Oh, yes.
You certainly
fucking can.

"What's your favorite
position?"

"CEO."

Lauren Conrad

So recommit.
Recommit as many times
as you need
to your well-being,
your dreams,
your spiritual health,
your workouts,
or your promises.
Recommit to
your self-belief.
Failure is an illusion
and the idea that you
can't start over will
do nothing but keep
you in a space of
sadness.
You can start over at
any time, at any
minute.
And this one feels
perfect.

Cara Alwill Leyba

Your gut knows
what's up.
Trust that bitch.

I think women
are very powerful
and I think we're more
powerful together
than separate.

Zendaya Coleman

You are allowed
to be both
a masterpiece
and a work
in progress,
simultaneously.

Sophia Bush

Don't let them treat
you like shit,
just because
you love them.

Mel Robbins

Maybe our girlfriends
are our
soul mates
and guys are just
people to have fun
with.

Carrie Bradshaw,
Sex and the City

Look closely
at the present
you are constructing.
It should look like
the future you are
dreaming.

Alice Walker

Life is tricky baby,
stay in your magic.

I'm not going to let
public opinion dictate
my own feelings about
myself.
I'm not going to
apologize for anything
I've done.

Madonna

Perspective is the most
important thing to
have in life.

Lauren Graham

I love it when women
love themselves.
I love it when women
are learning to love
themselves.
I love it when women
inspire other women to
love themselves.

alone or not
you gotta walk
forward

Cecilia Ahern

I knew I was lacking
love for myself
when I expected people
to recognize my
hurting
and make it a priority
to save me.
I needed to save me.

mia

It's really liberating
to say "no"
to shit you hate.

Hannah Horvath,
Girls

There is no limit
to what
we as women
can accomplish.

Michelle Obama

Darling,
you are a goddess.
And once you know
what that truly
means,
I pray for anyone
who tries to hurt you.

Change doesn't start
with cleaning out the
garage.
It starts with
cleaning out your
mind.

Sarah Knight

Think about where you
were last year.
Think about the things
that used to worry
you so much that no
longer consume your mind
and time.
The relationship that
wasn't healthy, the stress
of what this year would
be like, the things
you never thought
you would accomplish
but did...
all of those things
are worthy of being
grateful for, and are
beautiful reminders that
after everything
that happened,
you are going to be okay.

Morgan Harper Nichols

You want to come in my
life, the door is open.
You want to get out of
my life,
the door is open.
Just one request.
Don't stand
at the door,
you're blocking the
traffic.

I figure if a girl
wants to be a legend,
she should just go
ahead and be one.

Calamity Jane

Be your own artist,
and always be
confident in what
you're doing.
If you're not going
to be confident,
you might as well
not be doing it.

Aretha Franklin

Repeat every single
day:

I am worthy.
I am relentless.
I am enough.

I sat with my anger
long enough,
until she told me her
real name was grief.

It's interesting
how we often
can't see the ways
in which we
are being strong.

Lena Dunham

Just let go.
Let go of how you
thought your life
should be,
and embrace the life
that is trying to work
its way into your
consciousness.

Caroline Myss

It will never be
perfect.

Make it work.

-life

Shedding your armor
is brave.
Vulnerability
is beautiful.
Scars and
imperfections
and hours lived with
edges and grit
are stunning.

Own. It. All.

Katie Yackley Moore

Whatever makes you
feel the sun
from the inside out
chase that.

gemma troy

Slay your own dragons,
Princess.

Be happy with what
you have,
while working
for what you want.

Helen Keller

See how fast
this year passed?
You better stop
playing with
your life.

They tried to bury us.
They didn't know
we were seeds.

Mexican Proverb

Don't compromise
yourself.
You're all you've got.

Janis Joplin

I want every girl
to know
that her voice
can change the world.

Self-awareness
is probably the most
important thing
toward being a
champion.

Billie Jean King

You've got to spread
your light
like blazes
all across the sky.

Joni Mitchell

The soul should always
stand ajar,
ready to welcome the
ecstatic experience.

Emily Dickinson

Knowing what
must be done with
does away with fear.

Rosa Parks

We cannot complain
about the results
we don't get for the
work we didn't do.

Gina Truman

Stop getting
distracted by things
that have nothing
to do with your goals.

The woman you're
becoming will cost you
people, relationships,
spaces and material
things.
Choose her over
everything.

And it occurs to me
that maybe the reason
my mother was
so exhausted all the
time wasn't because
she was doing so much
but because she
was feeling so much.

Kelly Corrigan,
Glitter and Glue

Dreaming,
after all,
is a form of planning.

Gloria Steinem

Darling, you deserve
it all.
You deserve love
and peace and magic
and joy dancing
in your eyes.
You deserve hearty,
deep-belly laughter
and the right to let
those tears fall
and water the soil.
You deserve freedom
and goodness
and company and days
of bliss and quiet too.
You deserve you happy
and healed
and content and open.
So keep going,
darling.
Keep going.
Go realize into being
the life you deserve.

We need women who are
so strong they can be
gentle, so educated
they can be humble,
so fierce they can be
compassionate,
so passionate they can
be rational
and so disciplined
they can be free.

Kavita Ramdas

Perfection isn't what
matters.
In fact,
it's the very thing
that can destroy you...

Emily Giffin

Girl,
you already
have what it takes.

The Kind Initiative

When I stand before
God at the end
of my life,
I would hope that
I would not have
a single bit of talent
left,
and could say,
'I used everything
you gave me.'

Erma Bombeck

If you found out you
were dying, would you
be nicer, love more,
try something new?

Well, you are.
We all are.

How we handle
our fears
will determine where
we go with the rest
of our lives.

Judy Blume

Note to self:
None of us are getting
out of here alive,
so please stop treating
yourself like
an after thought.
Eat the delicious food.
Walk in the sunshine.
Jump in the ocean.
Say the truth that
you're carrying in
your heart like
hidden treasure.
Be silly. Be kind.
Be weird.
There's no time for
anything else.

Let's get free of the
idea that we can't go
after our dreams
because of how we look,
where we come from,
who we love or how old
we are...
We all have gifts
and we can either lock
into those gifts or act
like we don't exist.
You can't live your
dream
if you don't go after
it.

Lena Waithe

People will throw
stones at you.
Don't throw them back.
Collect them all
and build an empire.

Be true to your moral
compass.
Don't let anyone
convince you that just
because something's
always been done
a certain way,
it must be right.

Jodi Picoult

People show their true
colors,
unintentionally.
Pay attention.

Being human is having
to be both the one who
breaks and the one
who picks up the
broken pieces.
Sometimes at the
same time.

Emily McDowell

Falling down
is an accident.
Staying down
is a choice.

Never ever mistake
her silence for
weakness.
Remember that
sometimes
the air stills
before the onset
of a hurricane...

Nikita Gill

Look around you.
How many people do you
think are settling?
Probably a hell
of a lot.
People settle into okay
relationships, okay jobs,
okay friends, and an okay
life.
Why?
Because okay is
comfortable.
Okay pays the bills and
provides a warm
bed at night.
Some people are fine with
okay and guess what?
That's okay.
But okay
is not thrilling,
it isn't passion, it's not
life-changing or
unforgettable.
Okay is not the reason
you risk absolutely
everything you've got for
the smallest chance that
something absolutely
amazing could happen.

To watch people push
themselves further
than they think they
can,
it's a beautiful thing.

Abby Wambach

Don't for the love
of heaven let anybody
rush you
into anything.

Julia Child

Try to live every day
like Elle Woods after
Warner told her that
she wasn't smart
enough for law school.

You don't know this
new me;
I put back my pieces
differently.

High Poets Society

There is no limit
to how radiant, alive
and irresistible
you can be.

Rock bottom became
the solid foundation
on which I rebuilt
my life.

J.K. Rowling

This woman that I'm
becoming gives
me chills.
I'm obligated to move
differently.
I have work to do.

The minute you learn
to love yourself,
you won't want to be
anyone else.

Rihanna

Everybody has a home
team. It's the people
you call when you get
a flat tire or when
something terrible
happens. It's the
people who,
near or far,
know everything that's
wrong with you and
love you anyways.
These are the ones who
tell you their secrets,
who get themselves a
glass of water without
asking when they're
at your house.
These are the people
who cry when you cry.
These are your people,
your middle-of-the-
night,
no-matter-what people.

Watch for the people
whose eyes light up
when you talk about
your dream.
Those are the people
you keep.

Elizabeth Gilbert

Know what?
Bitches get stuff
done.

Tina Fey

The people making
you feel guilty for
going your own way
and choosing your own
life are simply trying
to keep you
in the chains
they are in.

Be thankful for every
heartbreak, for they
were planned.
They come into your
life just to reveal
another layer of
yourself to you,
and then leave.
Their purpose is
to shake you up, tear
apart your ego a little
bit, show you your
obstacles
and addictions,
break your heart open
so new light can get
in, make you
so desperate and out
of control that you
have to transform your
life.
And you do.

Resilience is
silent and deep,
like roots.
It doesn't announce
itself.
It doesn't explode
outward.
It doesn't fall.
It doesn't break.
It simply always is.
And you are.

Victoria Erickson

Those that don't got
it,
can't show it.
Those that got it,
can't hide it.

Zora Neale Huston

Don't judge yourself
by your past.
You don't live there
anymore.

You become.
It takes a long time.
That's why it doesn't
happen often to people
who break easily, or have
sharp edges, or who have
to be carefully kept.
Generally, by the time
you are Real, most of your
hair has been loved off,
and your eyes drop out
and you get loose in your
joints and very shabby.
But these things don't
matter at all, because
once you are Real you
can't be ugly, except
to people who don't
understand.

Margery Williams,
The Velveteen Rabbit

Some talk to you
in their free time,
and some free their
time to talk to you.
Learn the difference.

Find a group of people
who challenge
and inspire you,
spend a lot of time
with them,
and it will change
your life.

Amy Poehler

They say you're the
average of the 5
people you spend the
most time with.
Take that advice
to heart. Surround
yourself with those
who push you, cheer
for you, challenge
you and love you.
Surround yourself
with those who believe
the world
is a beautiful place,
those who are
courageous and those
who make you grow.

Sam Brown

Please, keep looking.
Not for a person,
but for your passion,
your love,
your courage,
your goals,
your dreams,
your happiness,
yourself.
Keep looking.
Explore yourself
before you explore
another.
Know your worth,
know yourself.
Only then will you
know what you need
over what you want.
You need yourself to
become your own.

Pretty is a lovely
thing to be called.

But have you tried out
bravery?

Pretty is the bones
that you are born
with.

Brave is what you
chose to do with them.

Katie Yackley Moore,
Happy Broken Crayons

I can do this,
I thought.
Then:
And even if I can't,
I have to.

'Why the fuck not me?'
should be your motto.

Mindy Kaling

Come on kid.
This is your dream.

I don't have to prove
anything to anyone,
I only have to follow
my heart
and concentrate
on what I want
to say to the world.

I run my world.

Beyonce

You don't have a right
to the cards you
believe you should
have been dealt.
You have an obligation
to play the hell out of
the ones you're
holding.

Cheryl Strayed

No apologizing today,
darling,
for who you are,
for how you see life,
for how you breathe.
No hiding either.
No shame.
You just be you.
The world will catch
up with your fire
eventually.

S.C Lourie

It's amazing what you
can get when you
quietly, clearly
and authoritatively
demand it.

Meryl Streep

It's all messy:
the hair, the bed,
the words, the heart.
Life.

You are the architect
of your
own happiness,

everyone else is
simply a visitor.

pavana

To heal a wound
you need to stop
touching it.

Imagine a life filled
with calling in
people who aren't
just her to trigger
your unhealed trauma
but instead to match
your joy, bliss,
passion and purpose.

Maryam Hasnaa

Women, like men,
should try to do
the impossible.
And when they fail,
their failure should
be a challenge
to others.

Amelia Earhart

We need to raise our
voices a little more,
even as they say to us,
'this is so
uncharacteristic
of you.'
Invisibility is not
a natural state for
anyone.

Mitsuye Yamada

My coach said I run
like a girl.
And I said if he ran
a little faster he
could too.

Mia Hamm

It took me quite a long
time to develop
a voice,
and now that
I have it,
I am not going
to be silent.

Madeleine Albright

But I don't want small
talk. Text me, and
without saying hello,
tell me why you got
so angry at your sister
this morning. Tell me why
you have a scar shaped
like Europe on the left
side of your neck.
Send me paragraphs about
the time you spent at
your grandmother's house
that one summer.
Call me when I'm half
asleep and tell me why
you believe in God.
Tell me about the first
time you saw your dad
cry. Go on for hours about
things that may not seem
important because I
promise that I'll be
hanging on every word
you say.
Tell me everything.
I don't want someone who
just talks about the
weather.

Each time women
gather in circles with
each other the world
heals a little more.

wildwomansisterhood

If one man can destroy
everything,
why can't one girl
change it?

Malala Yousafzai

I'm learning as I go
and most of the time
I'm a hot mess.
My tongue is
passionate and bold
and I have a habit of
letting my wild heart
pull me along before I
think it all through.
But I'm trying and I
think I'd rather be
a chaotic mess of
burning passion
than a perfectly
put together
coward.

Brooke Hampton

To all the little
girls,
never doubt that you
are valuable
and powerful
and deserving
of every chance
and opportunity
in the world to pursue
and achieve
your own dreams.

Hillary Clinton

I am not afraid.
I was born to do this.

Joan of Arc

I am not lucky.
You know what I am?
I am smart.
I am talented.
I take advantage of
the opportunities that
come my way and I work
really, really hard.

Don't call me lucky.
Call me a badass.

Shonda Rhimes

You're always one
decision away from
a totally different
life.

No matter what
happens in life,
be good to people.
Being good to people is
a wonderful legacy
to leave behind.

Taylor Swift

I've never met a woman
who is not strong.
They don't exist.

Diane Von Furstenberg

When you take time
to replenish your
spirit, it allows you
to serve others from
the overflow.
You cannot serve from
an empty vessel.

Eleanor Brown

Stop saying 'yes'
and 'ok'
when you be saying
'no thanks'
and 'fuck off.'

I know I changed baby.
That was the point.

#bossbabe

Don't be sorry.
Don't you cry.
It's enough
that you
tried.

Margo T. Rose,
The Words

I believe ambition
is not a dirty word,
it's believing
in yourself
and your abilities.
Imagine this: what
would happen if we
were all brave enough
to believe in our own
ability, to be a little
more ambitious.
I think the world
would change.

Reese Witherspoon

Assess.
Acquire.
Attain.
Accumulate.

Jennifer Novak,
The Real Houses of
Davidsonville

You're not supposed
to be happy
all the time.
Life hurts
and it's hard.
Not because you're
doing it wrong,
but because it hurts
for everybody.
Don't avoid the pain.
You need it.
It's meant for you.
Be still with it,
let it come, let it go,
let it leave you with
the fuel you'll burn
to get your work done
on this earth.

Glennon Doyle Melton

Stop telling girls
they can be anything
they want when they
grow up.
I think it's a mistake.
Not because they can't,
but because it would
have never occurred to
them they couldn't.

Sarah Silverman

both soft & fierce
can coexist
and still be powerful

Danielle Doby

That podcast?
Launch it.
That blog?
Start it.
That book?
Write it.
That idea?
Flesh it out.
That app?
Develop it.
That gift?
Put it to use.
That life?
Live it.

How many trot out
that tried cliché-
'I'm waiting for God to
open a door'-
and he is all,
'I love you but get
going, pumpkin,'
because usually
chasing that dream in
your heart
looks surprisingly
like work.

Jen Hatmaker

You're allowed to move
on with your life.
You're allowed to
change.
Don't hold on to who
you were just to please
others.

'Finding yourself'
is not really how it
works. You aren't
a ten-dollar bill in
last winter's coat
pocket. You are also
not lost. Your true
self is right there,
buried under cultural
conditioning, other
people's opinions,
and inaccurate
conclusions you drew
at a kid that became
your beliefs about who
you are. 'Finding
yourself' is actually
returning to yourself.
An unlearning, an
excavation,
a remembering who you
were before the world
got its hands on you.

Emily McDowell

Be a stiletto.
Lift other women up
and remind them that
they are fucking
badass.

When my children
remember their childhood,
I want only for them to
remember that their
mother gave it her all.
She worried too much, she
failed at times and she
did not always get it
right... but she tried her
hardest to teach them
about kindness, love,
compassion and honesty.
Even if she had to learn
it from her own mistakes
she loved them enough to
keep going, even when
things seemed hopeless,
even when life kicked her
down.
I want them to remember
me as the woman who
always got back up.

@soul-fully beautiful

Flower child, you are
about to bloom.

Buy a notebook.
Write down what you
want.
Write down what hurts
you.
Show it to someone you
love.
Save it for your
children.
Burn it in the
backyard.
Either way, go to bed
knowing that in some
way, those things are
out of you.

If someone is clawing
at the door to get out
of your house, do not
turn the deadbolt to
keep them in.
Do not contain them.
Turn the handle, love.
You have the courage
to set them and
yourself free.

Katie Yackley Moore

Examine what you
tolerate.

Better bitch
than mouse.

Ruth Bader Ginsburg

Life keeps moving.
But no matter where
you go you are made up
of your memories of
the moments that
pierce you.
No one can tell you
what's important
or what matters
or what you'll
remember for the rest
of your life.
Not even you.

Emma Straub

My motto these days
can basically be
summed up as:
I'm a grown ass woman,
and I'm not here for
your bullshit.

she was a wild child;
always stealing the
stars and getting
drunk on the souls
of earthbound misfits.

h. lynn

Brave girl,
you were made for far
more beautiful things.
Chaos is only
understood when it is
loved by the wild,
not the weak.

Having a dream is
what keeps you alive.

Mary Tyler Moore

Divorce isn't such a
tragedy.
A tragedy's staying in
an unhappy marriage,
teaching your
children the wrong
things about love.
Nobody ever died of
divorce.

Jennifer Weiner

Why not have a big life?

Emily Dickinson

Don't be intimidated
by what you don't
know.
That can be your
greatest strength
and ensure that you do
things differently
from everyone else.

Sara Blakely

Get it girl.

You know what's
really, powerfully
sexy?
A sense of humor.
A taste for adventure.
A healthy glow.
Hips to grab on to.
Openness. Confidence.
Humility. Appetite.
Intuition...
Smart-ass comebacks.
Presence. A quick wit.
Dirty jokes told by an
innocent looking
lady...
A woman who realizes
how beautiful she is.

Courtney E. Martin

The best kind of
friendships are fierce
lady friendships
where you
aggressively believe
in each other,
defend each other,
and think that
the other deserves
the world.

You can't be committed
to your bullshit and
to your growth.
It's one or the other.

So as you think about how
to raise your daughter
to be
a confident
and courageous woman-
sure of herself
and resilient under
pressure- begin
by considering where
you need to practice
a little more bravery
yourself.
Any time you tip toe
around an awkward
conversation,
allow someone treat you
poorly, avoid taking
a risk for fear of failure
or let other people's
opinions matter more
than your own,
you're missing an
important opportunity
to teach your daughter
how to be brave.

Margie Warrell

You will not always be
the smartest person in
the room, and you will
not always be
the strongest or the
funniest or the most
talented.
But you can always be
brave and you can
always be kind,
and these are the
things you should be
every minute of every
day for the rest of
your life.
Because yes, those
other things,
they're great things.

But these things are
better.

As for my girls, I'll
raise them to think
they breathe fire.

Jessica Kirkland

I don't need the
Prince Charming
to have my own
happy ending.

Katy Perry

Because this is my
life.
And that's the only
explanation you need.

We do not have to get
it together before
we show up.

Anne Lamott

Your fear
is full of shit.

Like a wild flower;
she spent her days
allowing herself
to grow, not many knew
of her struggle,
but eventually all;
knew of her light.

Nikki Rowe

One life.
Just one.

Why aren't we running
like we are on fire
towards our wildest
dreams?

Last night I was lying
in bed and I had an
idea for an outfit and
I just made myself get
up and sketch it real
fast then went back
to sleep.
I think it's when you
say 'I'm too tired,
I have to go to bed'
is when creativity
stops coming.

If God calls you,
pick up
the damn phone.

Lady Gaga

It became no longer
enough for her to live
on the surface.
Here's to knowing
people in the deep.

I can do things you
cannot,
you can do things I
cannot;
together we can do
great things.

Mother Teresa

The final forming of a
person's character lies
in their own hands.

Anne Frank

You are not a back-up plan.

Unfuck yourself.

Be who you were before
all that stuff
happened that dimmed
your fucking shine.

It is not the size of
the house that
matters.
It is the size of the
love inside that does.

Angie Moore

Everything has
beauty,
but not everyone sees
it.

Jennifer Lawrence

Of course I am not
worried about
intimidating men.
The type of man who
will be intimidated
by me is exactly the
type of man I have
no interest in.

Chimamanda Ngozi Adichie

She threw away all of
her masks,
and put on her soul.

Perhaps when you thought you weren't good enough the truth was that you were overqualified.

I sleep with
Fear every
now and then,
but I always
remind that
possessive
fucker that
he doesn't
own me.

Erin Van Vuren

You did not dig
your soul out of the
dark
to hand it to someone
else.

You'll need coffee
shops and sunsets
and roadtrips,
airplanes
and passports and new
songs and old songs,
but people more than
anything else.
You will need other
people and you will
need to be that other
person to someone else,
a living, breathing,
screaming invitation
to believe better
things.

Jamie Tworkowski

Grace carried me here
and by grace
I will carry on.

Please overuse your
intelligence.

It's sexy as hell.

My dear friend,
please just keep
treading. Keep riding the
inevitable waves. Stamp
your feet down with rage,
scream at the sky, shed
tears in the waves, bury
yourself in the sand if
you need to, just keep a
space that keeps you
breathing. Keep the space
that keeps you awake.
Keep the space that keeps
you feeling. Keep your
head toward the sun and
in due time you will feel
its warmth again.
Take all the time you
need.
When it comes to healing,
there should never be a
stopwatch involved.

Katie Yackley Moore

Don't underestimate
the healing power of
these three things...

Music.
The Ocean.
Stars.

Tonight,
I dream.

Tomorrow,
I do.

The very idea that
you're too kind,
too sensitive,
too emotional,
too enthusiastic,
too loving is bat shit
preposterous.

Meredith Marple

I'm living my
best life.
I ain't going back
and forth with you.

Someone I loved once
gave me a box full of
darkness.
It took me years to
understand that this
too,
was a gift.

Mary Oliver

There is no statute of
limitations on
starting over.
Re-invent yourself
every day. Be the girl
who walks barefoot
and listens to the
blues. Tomorrow,
wear a trench coat
and speak fierce
truths. Be a phoenix.
Be ashes. Burn down.
Resurrect.
Let go of the idea that
you must always be who
you have always been.

Slay. Girl. Slay.

She understood that
the hardest times
in life to go through
were when you were
transitioning from
one version of
yourself to another.

Sarah Addison Allen

The older I get, the
more I see how women
are described
as having gone mad,
when what they've
actually become is
knowledgeable
and powerful
and fucking furious.

Sophie Heawood

I'm standing in the
ashes of who I used
to be.

I hate small talks.
I wanna talk about
atoms, death, aliens,
sex, magic, intellect,
the meaning of life,
faraway galaxies,
the lies you've told,
your flaws,
your favorite scents,
your childhood,
what keeps you up at
night, your insecurity
and fears.
I like people with
depth, who speak with
emotion,
a twisted mind.

I don't want to know
'what's up.'

word porn

Start now.
Start where you are.
Start with fear.
Start with pain.
Start with doubt.
Start with hands
shaking.
Start with voice
trembling but start.
Start and don't stop.
Start where you are,
with what you have.
Just... start.

It's about being
alive & feisty
and not sitting down
and shutting up.

Even if people would
like you to.

Pink

Sometimes you just got
to give yourself the
pep talk.
Like hello you bad ass
bitch.
Don't be sad.
You're doing great.
Love you.

You are not required
to set yourself on fire
to keep other people
warm.

It takes years
as a woman to unlearn
what you have been
taught to be sorry
about.

Amy Poehler

find your equal,
not your whole.

mia

I was lucky enough to
have been to have been
to rock bottom before,
right?
So I know, for a fact,
that rock bottom is
always the beginning
of the newness.
It hurts and it's
painful, and then
there's the waiting-
where you don't know
what the hell is going
on and you don't think
any of it is going to
make sense and then,
there's the rising.

Glennon Doyle Melton

If you can't beat fear,
do it scared.

Ten years from now,
make sure you can say
that you chose
your life,
you didn't settle
for it.

this is not
your heart
breaking
my darling,
this is your
heart hatching,
shedding the shell
of who you
once were,
this is
your rebirth.

@axiom.attic

It's beautiful,
isn't it?

How it all hurts
but we never
give up.

The Word Virus

Know the difference
between those who stay
to feed the soil
and those who come to
grab the fruit.

To create one's own
world
takes courage.

Georgia O'Keeffe

And God help you if
you are a phoenix,
and you dare to rise
up from the ash.
A thousand eyes will
smolder with jealousy,
while you're just
flying past.

Ani DiFranco

Girls should never be
afraid to be smart.

Emma Watson

Edit your life
frequently and
ruthlessly.
It's your masterpiece
after all.

I'm a woman.
That means I break
hard. And mend like
a motherfucker;
all sexy and full of
heartbreakingly
beautiful scars.

Staceyann Chin

Don't let anyone rent
a space in your head,
unless they're
a good tenant.

Everything in life is
art. What you do.
How you dress, how you
love someone, and how
you talk.
Your smile and your
personality. What you
believe in, and all
your dreams.
The way you drink
your tea.
How you decorate your
home.
Or party.
Your grocery list.
The food you make.
How your writing
looks.
And the way you feel.
Life is art.

If I were asked to
give what I consider
the single most useful
bit of advice for all
humanity, it would be
this:
Expect trouble
as an inevitable part
of life, and when it
comes, hold your head
high. Look it squarely
in the eye, and say,
'I will be bigger than
you.
You cannot defeat me.'
Then, repeat to
yourself the most
comforting words of
all,
'This too will pass.'

Ann Landers

Sometimes standing
out can be our
beauty mark.

Sophia Moore (age 9)

Life goes by fast.
Enjoy it.
Calm down.
It's all funny.

Joan Rivers

The expert in
anything was once
a beginner.

Real courage is when
you know you're licked
before you begin,
but you begin anyway
and see it through,
no matter what.

Harper Lee

I have insecurities,
of course,
but I don't hang out
with anyone who points
them out to me.

Adele

There is no point at
which you can say,
'Well I'm successful
now.
I might as well take
a nap.'

Carrie Fisher

You come home,
make some tea,
sit down in your
armchair,
and all around there's
silence.
Everyone decides for
themselves whether
that's loneliness or
freedom.

She was no longer
anyone's puppet.
She cut her strings
free.

Katie Yackley Moore

You gotta stop
watering dead plants.

Who am I, you ask?
I am made from
all the people I've
encountered and all
the things I have
experienced.
Inside, I hold
the laughter of friends,
the arguments with
my parents,
the chattering of young
children and the warmth
from kind strangers.
Inside, there
are stitchings from
cracked hearts,
bitter words from heated
arguments,
music that gets me
through,
and emotions
I cannot convey.
I am made from all these
people and moments.
That is who I am.

Ming D. Liu

Be a real woman.
Support, encourage,
compliment and cheer
on fellow females,
both in business and
your personal life.
And do it all with an
inspiring amount
of love and grace.

To make a difference
in someone's life you
don't have to be
brilliant, rich,
beautiful, or perfect.
You just have to care.

Mandy Hale

my circle is small but
the love is
enormous and genuine.
it gets no better.

Alex Elle

No makes room for yes,
and who doesn't want
more room for that?

Kelly Corrigan

When you are truly
genuine, there will
invariably be people
who do not accept you.
And in that case, you
must be your own
badass self,
without apology.

Katie Goodman

Even the silence has a
story to tell you.
Just listen. Listen.

Jacqueline Woodson

When the dust settles.
And you can finally
look in the mirror.
At the Woman.
Who survived through
it all.
Through the failures.
Through the flaws.
You'll realize.
That even as fragile
as you are.
You're still
unbreakable.

What if you wake up
some day,
and you're 65, or 75,
and you never got your
memoir or novel written;
or you didn't go swimming
in warm pools and oceans
all those years because
your thighs were jiggly
and you had
a nice big comfortable
tummy; or you were just
so strung out
on perfectionism
and people-pleasing that
you forgot to have a big
juicy creative life,
of imagination
and radical silliness
and staring off into
space like when you were
a kid?
It's going
to break your heart.
Don't let this happen.

Anne Lamott

What's a queen without
her king?
Well,
historically speaking,
more powerful.

I'll be myself until
they fucking close the
coffin.

She never smoothed her
wild edges.
She never stopped writing
new chapters.
She fell.
She rose.
She danced.
She unraveled.
She let go.
She evolved.
She was a tangled mess.
She was strong.
She was fierce.
She was brave.
She was a badass.
The ocean was her
therapy.
Grace was her religion.
Imperfection was her
backbone.
Forgiveness was her
freedom.
She lived like there
would never be enough
time.
She lived like there was
fire in her veins.

She lived.

Katie Yackley Moore

a wise woman once said
'fuck this shit'
and she lived happily
ever after.

the end

acknowledgements:

I am crazy grateful to all the fierce
warriors in my life.
Thank you to my children, Lucy, Niko,
Sophia and Micah who always say the best
things and only once did I have to take
one of you to the ER while I was working
on this book.
Thank you to my mom and dad for their
relentless belief in me.
Thank you to Juls for being my soul mate.
Thank you to Greg and Tim for being the
best big brothers a girl could hope for.
Thank you to the hornets for helping me
stand on my heels again, for my soul
sisters Nicky, Angie and Brenda for being
my therapy and for my Roanoke girls,
Carly, Christine, Emily, Jess, Kara and
Megan for the laughter.
Thank you to my nieces and nephews, I
promise to write you a book with fewer
swear words.
Thank you to my family both by blood or
by bond near and far and to all I know
who I can reach out to any day, any time-
you are to the moon; I would need two
more lifetimes to thank you for all that
you have given me.
Thank you to all the women quoted in this
book for having the most powerful words.

about the author:

Katie Yackley Moore is a writer and real estate agent with Keller Williams Flagship and works with one of her favorite humans, Jennifer Novak on The Real Houses of Davidsonville Team.
She has written for Scary Mommy, HuffPost Parents, Mamalode, Chesapeake Family Life Magazine and Baltimore Real Producers.
You can find her on Instagram @katieyackleymoore, on Facebook @thenakedmomma and @therealhousesofdavidsonville.

She lives a happy and imperfect life outside of Annapolis with her four children.